Itty Bitty Bella Loves the Yellow Eyed Monster

Author Linda Floyd

Illustrated by Linda Floyd

It was a beautiful day, the sun was shining, and there was a soft, gentle breeze.

Bella was so excited to go outside and play.

She jumped out of her tree house and started picking wildflowers.

There were all kinds of colors. Bella wanted to make a pretty bouquet for Blue.

She was dancing and singing a song,

"Pink, yellow and blue, Sweetheart. I love you."

All of a sudden, out of the corner of her eye, Bella saw a yellow-eyed monster!

Bella tried to hide behind the tree, but the monster was watching her.

Bella prayed, "God, please help me get to Dad's house!"

She started to run, but she ended up tripping over a rock and falling.

Bella was afraid that she would not be able to get away. She had to find Dad for help!

Bella thought this monster could take over the world!

Bella was terrified!

Bella ran into Dad's house yelling,

"Dad! Dad! Help! I need help! There's a monster in the pond! It almost got me and ate me for dinner!"

Mom, Brandon, and Meggie came downstairs.

"What's going on, Bella? Dad is not home right now," said Mom.

"I need Dad! He has to help get the monster out of the pond," replied Bella.

Mom told Bella that there are no monsters.

But Brandon and Meggie thought differently.

Brandon said to Bella, "Come on. Let's go outside and try to find the monster."

"I am afraid," said Bella. "He has huge, yellow, glaring eyes and a great big mouth! He could swallow me in one bite!"

Meggie said, "We will hunt this monster down and catch him! Then Dad can put him in a cage and take him to 'Monster Land' and set him free with all the other monsters."

Can Dad do that without being eaten? Wondered, Bella.

Bella, Brandon, and Meggie all slowly walked out the door. Brandon had his binoculars so he could see far away with them.

Meggie and Bella held each other's hands tightly, so if the monster tried to get them, they would be able to run away together.

All of a sudden, Bella spotted the big yellow eyes; she said, "There he is! See him? His eyes are sticking up out of the water!"

"Oh, I do see him," said Brandon. "Run, everyone! The monster is getting out of the pond! RUN!!!!"

Blue came flying out of the treehouse and caught up with Bella, Brandon, and Meggie.

Blue asked, "What's going on? Why are you running and screaming?"

Bella was talking so fast that Blue could not understand a word she was saying. "Okay Bella, calm down! Tell me slowly, what's wrong?"

Bella explained that this monster tried to eat her, that she was able to get away and had run to Dad's house for help. But, unfortunately Dad was not at home. Brandon, Meggie and I are on a monster hunt to catch him and have Dad take him to 'Monster Land.'

Blue giggled, she tried not to laugh out loud. Blue said, "There are no monsters in the pond."

Ziggy and Buzzy heard all the yelling, and they came out to see if they could help.

Ziggy asked, "Is everything okay?"

"No!" said Bella. "There's a monster in the pond, and he's going to take over the world! We have to get Dad to catch him and take him to Monster Land."

Buzzy flew back over the pond, looking for this monster. All of a sudden he saw this huge yellow-eyed monster staring at him through the water.

Buzzy yelled, "MONSTER!!!!!!!"

Mom came outside and told everyone that Dad was on his way home. He would make sure everyone was safe.

They all went inside the house and into the living room, where they remained with their faces stuck to the window, while they carefully watched to see if the monster was coming out of the pond.

Bella said, "Sparky and the aphids are still out there. I hope Dad gets home soon."

"Me too," said Meggie. "I know Dad will catch that monster and then we will all be safe."

Bella saw Sparky and the aphids flying around the pond. "Oh no," she said. "The monster is going to eat them!"

They all started tapping on the window, trying to get Sparky's attention.

All of a sudden, the gigantic yellow-eyed monster jumped out of the pond, and Sparky and the aphids disappeared.

Bella was yelling, "Oh no, he ate them!"

Everyone became afraid because now they all knew that Bella had seen an enormous yellow-eyed monster for real.

Dad pulled up and saw all of them glued to the window staring at the pond. He scratched his head and walked down there.

Bella was yelling, "Dad, no!" "Don't go down there! The monster already ate Sparky and the aphids!"

All of a sudden, Dad disappeared, and everyone thought the monster had eaten Dad too!

They all were crying and wondering what was going to happen next.

Mom said, "It's okay, everyone. Dad is still down there. You just can't see him because of the trees."

Brandon jumped up and said, "I will not let this monster eat anyone else. I am going out there to catch him."

"Me too," said Meggie. "I am mad now!"

Bella was able to find strength, and she ran outside with Brandon and Meggie.

Then Dad came walking up the path. Everyone ran and grabbed Dad and held on to him very tight.

Meggie said, "Dad, I thought the monster ate you. He ate Sparky and the aphids."

Dad started laughing and said, "There are no monster's in the pond, Sparky, is down there playing with our new friend Worry Wart."

Bella ran down and saw the huge yellow-eyed monster playing Patty Cake with the aphids. The monster looked up and stared at Bella. All of a sudden he took a great big leap and landed right on top of her.

Bella started screaming, "Help, he's going to eat me! Help, get him off of me!"

Then she heard him say,

"Hi! My name is Worry Wart. I just moved here last night from the 'Land of Unusual'."

Bella opened up her eyes and asked him, "What are you?"

"I am a bullfrog."

"So, you're not a monster?" asked Bella.

Worry Wart giggled and said, "No I am not a monster."

"What do you eat?" asked Bella.

"I love pizza," said Worry Wart.

Bella giggled and said, "I love pizza too!"

Bella asked Dad, Can we have pizza tonight, with lots of cheese, please?"

Worry Wart, Brandon, Meggie, and Blue all agreed with Bella that pizza sounded great.

"Okay," said Dad. "Let's make some pizzas. Who wants to help?"

"I do!" replied Bella.

"Me too!" said Meggie.

Everyone ran into the house to help make the pizza's. Meggie grated the cheese; Brandon was making the dough; Bella sat on the counter with a spoon spreading the tomato sauce. Mom was baking the pizza's, and Dad was taking them out of the oven. Blue started serving, and Worry Wart was ready to eat.

Bella yelled, "Wait! Don't eat yet; we have to pray!"

Bella was very curious about Worry Wart's name, so she asked him, "Do you worry?"

Worry Wart told Bella when he was little it was a nickname he'd been given because he was always worried about fitting in and not being loved.

Bella said, "Oh, Worry Wart we love you!" Everyone agreed and ran over and hugged him. Worry Wart was so happy that he found a new family.

Dad said, "Let's have a campfire."

"Yay! Can we roast marshmallows?" asked Bella.

"Sure we can," said Mom.

Everyone gathered around the campfire roasting marshmallows and sharing their story with Worry Wart about how they had thought he was a monster. They were all laughing and having a fun time.

Blue said, "Bella, it's time to go home. It's getting late."

Bella hugged everyone and told them she loved them very much.

Bella said, "It was wonderful to meet you, Worry Wart. Now that I know you're not a monster, we can have lots of fun."

Blue got Bella's bath started. Bella hopped into her bubble bath.

Bella said, "I wonder if Worry Wart will take me for a ride across the pond?"

Blue said, "I am sure he will, and you will have lots of fun playing with him."

Blue tucked Bella into bed.

Bella told Blue, "I am sure glad that Worry Wart is not a monster."

"Me too!" giggled Blue.

Bella thanked God that there were no monster's in the pond. She blessed all of her family and friends. Bella fell fast asleep and started dreaming of how much fun Worry Wart and her would have tomorrow.

The End

Linda Floyd was born in Puerto Rico. She lives with her husband David in Albany, Oregon. They have four children and four grandchildren between them. Linda Floyd worked in the health field helping children with special needs. She attended Nazarene Bible College. Linda became an ordained Minister in 2002. She also is a licensed Drug and Alcohol Counselor. Ever since she was a little girl, Linda has been a storyteller. She has had all kinds of characters playing in her head. Linda's wild imagination brought a lot of these characters to life when she had her own children. She began writing stories for her children and for her grandchildren. The character "Bella" became a part of Linda's family. Bella is spoken about as if she is really alive amongst Linda's family and friends. They all have gotten involved talking about Bella and asking Linda "What is Bella doing today?" Linda gets inspired by sitting outside, looking at the large oak trees and pond in her yard. Bella and her friends have come alive in the Floyd household.

Made in the USA
San Bernardino, CA
14 October 2017